RUBANK BOOK OF TROMBONE/BARITONE B.C. SOLOS
EASY TO INTERMEDIATE LEVEL

INCLUDED
lings
mpaniments

PLAYBACK+
Speed • Pitch • Balance • Loop

CONTENTS

Allerseelen...R. Strauss/trans. Harold L. Walters — 16

Berceuse...G. Concone/trans. Wm. Gower — 10

Carnival Of Venice (Air Varie)...Henry W. Davis — 4

Chartreuse...Frank D. Cofield — 14

Dawn Of Spring...Clair W. Johnson — 12

Friends (Waltz Caprice)...Clay Smith — 11

March Of A Marionette...C. Gounod/arr. Harold L. Walters — 6

Meditation...G. Concone/trans. Wm. Gower — 9

Red Canyons...Clair W. Johnson — 8

Saraband...G. F. Handel/trans. Wm. Gower — 3

To access recordings and PDF accompaniments visit:
www.halleonard.com/mylibrary

4873-0318-0289-7427

ISBN 978-1-4950-6511-8

7777 W. BLUEMOUND RD. P.O. BOX 13819 MILWAUKEE, WI 53213

Visit Hal Leonard Online at
www.halleonard.com

Saraband

Trombone/Baritone B.C.

G.F. Handel
Transcribed by Wm. Gower

Carnival Of Venice

Air Varie

Trombone/Baritone B.C.

Henry W. Davis

Gran gusto

mf

Piano

Cadenza

Piano

Con grazia

Piano

mf

accel.

f

rit.

March Of A Marionette

Trombone/Baritone B.C.

Chas. Gounod
Arranged by Harold L. Walters

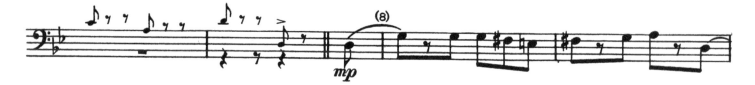

8

Red Canyons

Trombone/Baritone B.C.

Clair W. Johnson

Meditation

Trombone/Baritone B.C.

G. Concone
Transcribed by Wm. Gower

Andante con moto

Berceuse

Trombone/Baritone B.C.

G. Concone
Transcribed by Wm. Gower

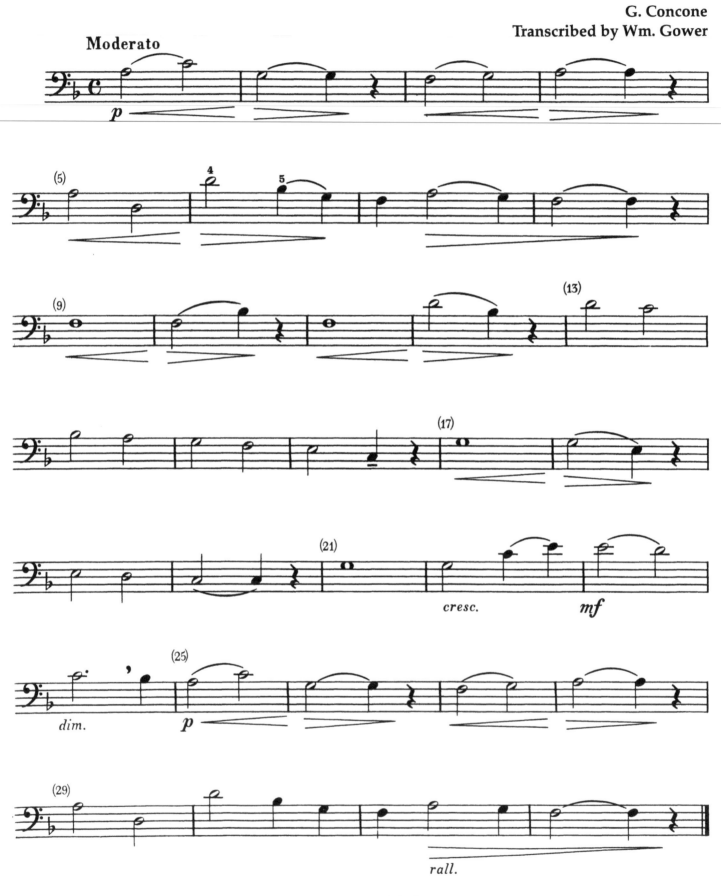

Friends

Waltz Caprice

Trombone/Baritone B.C.

Clay Smith

Dawn Of Spring

Trombone/Baritone B.C.

Clair W. Johnson

Trombone/Baritone B.C.

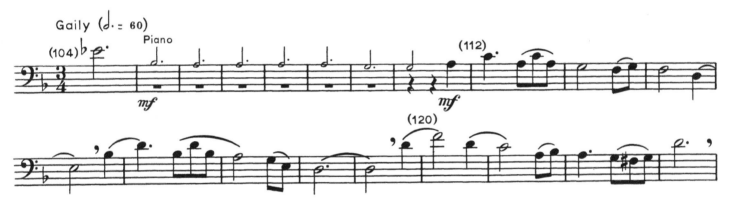

14

Chartreuse

Trombone/Baritone B.C.

Frank D. Cofield

Trombone/Baritone B.C.

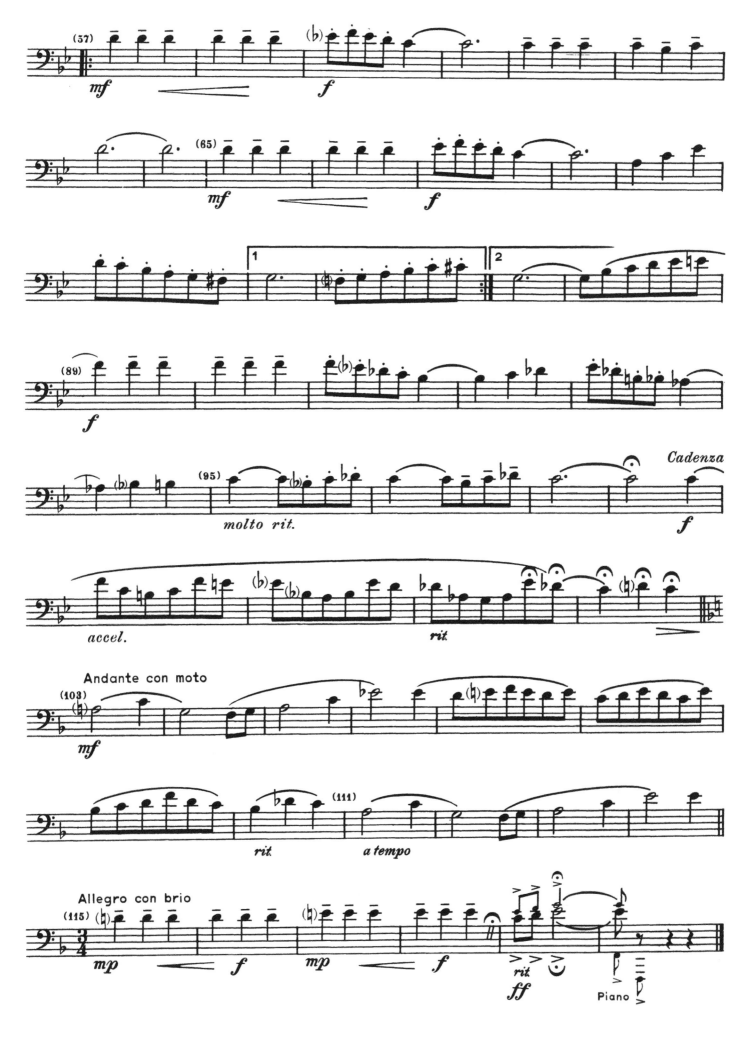

Allerseelen

Op. 10, No. 8

Trombone/Baritone B.C.

Richard Strauss
Transcribed by Harold L. Walters